YOUR KNOWLEDGE HAS VALUE

Mark Schauer

Precis Critique of Aphra Behn's "The Rover"

GRIN Verlag

Bibliografische Information der Deutschen Nationalbibliothek:

Die Deutsche Bibliothek verzeichnet diese Publikation in der Deutschen National-
bibliografie; detaillierte bibliografische Daten sind im Internet über http://dnb.d-
nb.de/ abrufbar.

Dieses Werk sowie alle darin enthaltenen einzelnen Beiträge und Abbildungen
sind urheberrechtlich geschützt. Jede Verwertung, die nicht ausdrücklich vom
Urheberrechtsschutz zugelassen ist, bedarf der vorherigen Zustimmung des Verla-
ges. Das gilt insbesondere für Vervielfältigungen, Bearbeitungen, Übersetzungen,
Mikroverfilmungen, Auswertungen durch Datenbanken und für die Einspeicherung
und Verarbeitung in elektronische Systeme. Alle Rechte, auch die des auszugsweisen
Nachdrucks, der fotomechanischen Wiedergabe (einschließlich Mikrokopie) sowie
der Auswertung durch Datenbanken oder ähnliche Einrichtungen, vorbehalten.

Imprint:

Copyright © 2012 GRIN Verlag GmbH
Druck und Bindung: Books on Demand GmbH, Norderstedt Germany
ISBN: 978-3-656-46022-0

This book at GRIN:

http://www.grin.com/en/e-book/230267/precis-critique-of-aphra-behn-s-the-rover

GRIN - Your knowledge has value

Der GRIN Verlag publiziert seit 1998 wissenschaftliche Arbeiten von Studenten, Hochschullehrern und anderen Akademikern als eBook und gedrucktes Buch. Die Verlagswebsite www.grin.com ist die ideale Plattform zur Veröffentlichung von Hausarbeiten, Abschlussarbeiten, wissenschaftlichen Aufsätzen, Dissertationen und Fachbüchern.

Visit us on the internet:

http://www.grin.com/

http://www.facebook.com/grincom

http://www.twitter.com/grin_com

Critique one

Anita Pacheco's 1998 article "Rape and the Female Subject in Aphra Behn's *The Rover*" uses "the central role which rape plays in... struggles to escape patriarchal devaluation" by female characters in *The Rover* as its thesis. (Pacheco 323)Pacheco holds that rape psychology was endemic in the dramatic conventions of the Restoration, and the objectified status of women made rape acutely likely absent the protection of a male protector. (323) Though during this period in history the legal definition of rape was in transition from a property crime against men to a personal crime against a woman, studies show that prosecutions were infrequent and usually against lower class men who violated young upper class girls. (Pacheco 324)

The biggest weakness in Pacheco's supporting argument is that there was no actual rape in *The Rover*. A more precise thesis would have been that the nebulous, but ever-present *threat* of rape buttressed patriarchal dominance: it was from this threat that fathers and brothers achieved the authority to protect, and gallants achieved the authority to protect upper class women from violations from members of the lower class. Of course, the actual possibility of rape was a necessary component of this power, and, as we see in *The Rover* when Don Pedro is willing to participate in a gang rape of masked Florinda, patriarchal society meant that a man could be both protector and predator. (This is one reason Hellena is not concerned by Willmore's attempted rape of her sister on multiple occasions.) Class lines and possession by a suitably high-ranking male is what afforded a woman protection from this threat, though, as Pacheco pointedly observes, "none of the male characters, Belvile included, can invariably tell ladies from whores." (Pacheco 333) To this writer, most of the characters in the play are cartoonishly infantile, something that Pacheco doesn't mention in her analysis.

Pacheco goes into great detail documenting how female bodies were in this time period objects for and against which male competitive struggles took place. She implies that the ideal male prerogative of this time was to live governed by unrestrained id, and that frustration ensues when this is impeded, such as it was for Willmore by Angellica's high price and his inability to pay. The violence breaks out, however, when another man does have the means to get what Willmore cannot. It could be further argued that Blunt's rage was occasioned less by his being duped by a prostitute than by a male pimp's complicity in the scheme and his subsequent humiliation in front of other men.

Critique Two

"Ethics, Politics, and Heterosexual Desire in Aphra Behn's *The Rover*", written by Elizabeth Kraft and published in 2001, interprets Hellena and Willmore's relationship from an ethical perspective. Taking the Biblical *Song of Songs* as the model of ethical sexuality, Kraft asserts that Hellena and Willmore engage in, "a chiasmus of double desire, an erotic union founded not on possession but on respect for Otherness... ." (Kraft 2) Kraft believes that the two characters' banter and discovery of common traits indicates a mutuality of desire in which both parties remain subjects, and sees a similar dynamic between Harriet and Dorimant in *The Man of Mode*. The conflict of the play, says Kraft, is the characters' grappling with the, "sociopolitical impediments to the ethical ideal," which is a substantial and rather contradictory addition to Pacheco's earlier interpretation.

It seems there is much in the play that doesn't support Kraft's argument, but those elements— Willmore's interactions with other women, the repeated rape attempts against Florinda—are minimized to a surprising degree. Kraft characterizes the attempted gang rape of Florinda by a group of men that includes her brother as, "reminiscent of a Marx Brothers routine," and opines that the rape scenes have, "less to do with male predatory violence than masculine animality, baseness, buffoonery." (Kraft 10) More astonishingly, Kraft interprets the scenes as, "argu(ing) for the need for female wit, self-direction, and focused desire but they do not establish the woman as victim." (Kraft 10) Florinda's desire seems pretty focused on Belvile throughout the play, and Kraft doesn't elaborate on how she thinks a wittier Florinda might have more successfully deterred her would-be rapists. While her interpretation of Willmore's exchanges with Angellica as being verbal power struggles is self-evident, her implication that Willmore's banter with Hellena is completely without such vying for control are not convincing.

Kraft deserves praise for finding in *The Rover* both elements that are of the time in which it was produced and that transcend the mores and circumstances of the era. Her conception of Willmore and Hellena's relationship is idealistic, but for one who disparages those who, "appropriate texts to shore up (their) own notions and political concerns," Kraft certainly seems to stretch the characters in *The Rover* more than slightly. Her contention that ethics do not necessarily equate with morality and calls for modern readers to uncouple their modern values from their consciousness while reading the play do not entirely shore up her interesting, but insufficient interpretation. Nonetheless, the piece is a valuable evolution in consciousness about Behn's work.

Critique Three

Kraft exhorted modern readers of *The Rover* to approach the work with enough historical imagination to view the play through the eyes of an audience member of the late 17th century, and Pilar Zozaya's "Representing women in Restoration England: A reassessment of Aphra Behn's *The Rover*", published in 2003, attempts to reconstruct the culture of that era with several pointed examples of English society's misogyny toward Behn and a recapping of the history of the theater in the years following Cromwell. Zozaya portrays the Restoration world as one of deep ambivalence: female actors, for example, were putatively allowed to improve the moral tone of the theater. (Zozaya 102) Women, however, were likewise considered to be "'natural imbeciles' who due to their bad temper could make men's lives utterly miserable." (Zozaya 104) Female actors (and playwrights) found it more difficult to achieve recognition from critics, and were considered of a similar social station to prostitutes. In short, "no woman could publicly expose and sell her mind without turning her body into that of a whore." (Zozaya 107) That Behn was the second-most prolific playwright of the era and favored by the king did not diminish this perception.

As for the play itself, Zozaya focuses on carnivalesque and political aspects, saying that, "Behn works on several levels... satirizing the figure of the male libertine; presenting a critique of female commodification; exposing the period's sexual politics; and even scorning Whig politics." (Zozaya 112) Zozaya gives a more in-depth comparison of *The Rover* and *Thomaso*, and explores cross-dressing by Hellena and Angellica as both empowering and further objectifying women. More interestingly, she zeroes in on the economic realities of the period, which both determined social identity and allowed women to be only wives or nuns—if a woman was neither, she was automatically a whore. (Zozaya 116) Zozaya agrees with Diamond that Angellica's relationship with Willmore was an attempt to free herself from the exchange economy and, "authenticate herself, to step out of the paintings, to be known not by her surface but by her depth." (Zozaya 119) Unfortunately, the only path open to Angellica was a relationship with an inconstant rover.

Zozaya sees Behn's play as objecting to the shallow constructs of society, class, and economic standing.

Critique Four

Cynthia Lowenthal's 2008 article, "Two Female Playwrights of the Restoration: Aphra Behn and Susanna Centlivre", widens Zozaya's consideration of both misogyny in Restoration culture and the historical significance of Behn by comparing and contrasting her work with that of Susanna Centlivre, the most popular female playwright of the era immediately following the Restoration. She also more explicitly points out the double standard that admired male characters that don disguises to dupe people into getting what they want, but condemned female characters for similar behavior. Thus, Centlivre's *Bold Stroke for a Wife* was, "less edgy, less anxiety-producing, and less provocative" than *The Rover*. (Lowenthal 1-2) Lowenthal argues that, as virtually the only female playwright accepted in their respective eras, both embodied the cultural norms of their day. As such, the Restoration's more libertine political economy was reflected in Behn's work. In this, Lowenthal's conception of Behn is more in line with Pacheco's than Kraft's. Lowenthal believes that both playwrights adhered to dominant social mores in their work and represented women as besieged by patriarchy, though Centlivre's was much more cautious than Behn's, as they usually feature blander, less witty female characters. (Lowenthal 7) They are also less romantic and more pragmatic, and Lowenthal introduces evidence that the post-Restoration period had less male violence than the Restoration.

The difficulty with Lowenthal's thesis of cultural change—that Centlivre's masculine heroes, "want to marry, not to bed, the women they love,"—is that marriage was shown as a proper destination for both gallants and female characters in every Restoration play we're thus far studied, including *The Rover*. In fact, it seems Dorimant in *The Man of Mode* used many of Sir Charles' tactics from *The Busie Body* in his efforts to win Harriet. The principle difference in male characters is Sir Charles' monogamy, his willingness to impersonate multiple characters, and his efforts being aimed at men, not women.

Lowenthal's linking Agellica Bianca and Ann Lovely was counterintuitive and a significant addition to the consideration of both periods.

Critique Five

"Subverting Hierarchy and Vying For Agency: Mistresses and Maidservants in Pix's *The Beau Defeated* and Behn's *The Rover*", a 2009 article by Rita Kondrath, uses these texts to explore the relationships between maids and mistresses, which were portrayed in a way that, "subvert(ed) the class hierarchy upon which such employment is based." (Kondrath 31) Maids in both plays are shown not merely taking orders from their mistresses, but actively advising and even supervising them. Kondrath asserts more strongly than the previous four scholars that both plays do not entirely reflect the dominant mores of the day.

Whereas other scholars have discussed at length the degree to which the physical structure of Restoration theater houses influenced the plays that were staged, Kondrath identifies the wide socioeconomic gamut of the theater's audience as a factor that period playwrights exploited. Kondrath believes that Behn and Pix took advantage of the demographics to introduce a revolutionary variety of strong women who subverted typical class and gender roles: self-possessed and intelligent servants and independent widows. Given that female playwrights were already associated with prostitutes, it was particularly courageous for Behn to, "elevate the servant to a position of respectability." (Kondrath 44) Kondrath's thesis is similar to that of Kraft, and contradicts Lowenthal, Pacheco and Zozaya.

Some readers might view Kondrath's supporting evidence as less indicative of equality and more a deeply rooted slave mentality on the part of the servants. Clearly the maids do not share the same privileges and advantages of their mistresses, even if the latter are oppressed relative to men, and thus it seems perverse for a character like Moretta or Betty to use words like "our" when discussing the mistress' problems. This could just as likely said out of pragmatic necessity than genuine concern. If anything, the upper class audience members likely wished they, too, could have servants as docile and caring as these, and saw the portrayals as more fanciful than revolutionary or subversive.

Works Cited

Pacheco, Anita. "Rape and the Female Subject in Aphra Behn's 'The Rover.'" English Literary History. (65:2): 1998. 323-45.

Kraft, Elizabeth. "Ethics, Politics, and Heterosexual Desire in Aphra Behn's 'The Rover.'" *Essays in Theatre/Etudes Théâtrales* (19:2): 2001. 111-25.

Zozaya, Pilar. "Representing Women in Restoration England: A Re-Assessment of Aphra Behn's 'The Rover.'" *Re- Shaping the Genres: Restoration Women Writers*. Ed. Zenón Luis-Martinez and Jorge Figueroa-Dorrego. Bern, Switzerland: Peter Lang, 2003. 99-122.

Lowenthall, Cynthia. "Two Female Playwrights of the Seventeenth Century: Aphra Behn and Susana Centlivre." *A Companion to Restoration Drama*. Ed. Susan J. Owen. Oxford: Blackwell Press, 2008. 396-411.

Kondrath, Rita Alison. "Subverting Hierarchy and Vying for Agency: Mistresses and Maidservants in Pix's 'The Beaux Defeated' and Behn's 'The Rover.'" *The Public's Open to Us All: Essays on Women and Performance in Eighteenth-Century England*. Ed. Laura Engel. Newcastle upon Tyne, England: Cambridge Scholars, 2009. 30-54.